The Piano Love Affair

Written by Jack Williams

as told by Charlie Brakebill

with a Foreword by Fred Brown

Periploi Press

NASHVILLE

© 2014 Jack Williams, Knoxville, TN
Published by Periploi Press, Nashville, TN
Second printing 2015

ISBN 978-0-9830115-4-5
LOC Control Number: 2014954922

Foreword by Fred Brown, author and
retired senior writer, the *Knoxville News-Sentinel*
Cover design: Kristin Williams, Knoxville, TN
Text design: Dariel Mayer

French piano photo on cover by Jack Williams,
courtesy of Michael Stinnett,
Antique Piano Shop, Friendsville, TN

Foreword

This story began on a rooftop in Rennes, France, 1944. Charlie Brakebill's generation of Americans had answered their nation's call in World War II by the hundreds of thousands, eventually building to millions. They saved the world from fascism, Nazism, evil dictatorships, and fostered one of the greatest economic recoveries in world history.

It is not by chance that Brakebill, nineteen at the time, and his era of American youth is known as "The Greatest Generation." They were spectacular in their achievements, during World War II and upon their return home, where they picked up their lives, earned college degrees on the GI Bill, and turned America into the greatest nation the world had ever witnessed.

When they arrived in Europe, some barely out of their teenage years, they faced the best Germany and Italy could throw at them. They landed on the crystalline beaches of Normandy and fought all the way to the Rhineland, stopping only to bury their dead.

They invaded desolate and disease-inducing tropical islands in the South Pacific and pushed the Japanese back to Japan. Many had returned home from the Victory in Europe and were preparing to finish the job when U.S. President Harry S. Truman made the truly dramatic decision to drop the first atomic weapon in history on the Japanese, ending World War II for good.

Charlie Brakebill, a country boy from Madisonville,

TN, was in the group of young men who returned from Europe with the burden of knowing that the war in the Pacific was not over and that they would be among those training to invade the Japanese archipelago. Had the U.S. invaded Japan's mainland, more than a million American casualties were predicted. Every American solider preparing for that invasion was aware of the casualty estimates.

The Atomic Bomb, first Little Boy on Hiroshima and then Fat Man on Nagasaki, was the vivid climax to the war's finality.

But for Charlie Brakebill, there was another emotion gnawing at him. His heart held a secret desire, but he realized that he had to go home, coloring a very human backstory to Charlie Brakebill's war history.

And that is what this book is about, war and love in a time of desperation and uncertainty.

The English had a classic saying about the American soldier: "overpaid, overfed, oversexed, and over here." There were hundreds of wartime "GI Brides," and marriages, and Charlie Brakebill came very close to having quite a different life than the one he found after the war's end, as this book details.

Jack Williams, former Vice President for Development and Alumni Affairs and Senior Adviser to the University of Tennessee president, is a longtime Brakebill friend. An accomplished photographer, once Williams learned of Charlie's wartime love story, he realized he had to write about it and to photograph the account, a kind of wartime memoir that could serve as a template for thousands of young Americans and young women of Europe during the anxiety and desperate hours of war.

That story is this book, the *The Piano Love Affair*,

about the relationship between Charlie Brakebill and the Brittany-born Anthelmette Guillard.

It is a beautiful love story and will bring back memories for veterans and their families alike, as it did for Charlie Brakebill.

While in Brittany, Charlie by chance glimpsed a stunning French girl and was immediately struck by her charm, attractiveness, and intelligence. She was studying pharmacy and living with her parents in war-ravaged Rennes.

In November 1944, Brakebill's unit was replacing a bombed-out roof on a building near the Rennes railway station, when Brakebill and members of his crew watched as a French family struggled to pull a piano up two stories and then through French doors on a second-floor apartment building near the building the Americans were repairing.

Brakebill quickly rounded up several of the soldiers who hoisted the piano into the apartment and then returned to work on the roof. But Brakebill held up a bit. He had spotted a beautiful young woman in the apartment as her family watched the soldiers complete the job.

It was then that Brakebill met the Guillard family—mother, father, grandmother, and Anthelmette, the daughter. Over the next several weeks Brakebill got to know the family and Anthelmette while working on the roof.

She was a pharmacy student at the University of Rennes. Her family had fled the French Port of Lorient when the Germans arrived so that she could continue her education.

As their friendship developed, Brakebill began purposely stalling the roof project so that he might get to know Anthelmette better.

With his Army base only about three miles distant from Anthelmette's home, Brakebill had been able to visit weekly or send letters to Anthelmette. She responded with letters or notes.

The two also began to take long walks in Thabor Gardens in Rennes. They sat at a bench along the garden's brick wall, their special place.

This was the beginning of *The Piano Love Affair*.

And that's where this story begins, on a rooftop in Rennes.

—Fred Brown
Knoxville, Tennessee
July 2014

The Piano Love Affair

On September 15, 1944, the USS Wakefield lifted anchor and sailed from the Boston docks for an eight-day voyage across the treacherous Atlantic Ocean, transporting 9,000 American soldiers and sailors to Liverpool, England, a large port on Britain's western coast. The quick deployment of Americans was set for Normandy and the French interior. Before the start of World War II, the renamed USS Wakefield was the Luxury Liner Manhattan. Stripped of any luxuries, the newly christened USS Wakefield was retrofitted with bunks "five deep" that provided about six inches of space between a man's head and the above bunkmate's butt when soldiers settled in for a night of rest. Untold adventures awaited sleepers if someone became seasick during the night. Men ate their meals while standing up. To say that things were overcrowded would be an underestimation of the packed and crowded scene aboard the USS Wakefield.

All these experiences awaited Corporal Charles F. Brakebill, a nineteen-year-old native of Madisonville, TN, as he stood on deck and watched the Boston skyline disappear into the distance. Before pulling out to sea, he and a friend, Ed Boling, and a few others had a chance to "see Boston" before heading to Europe, relieving some of their anxiety about what was to come. They had already seen some historical sites and even visited the Old Howard Theatre, a famous burlesque house. In fact, they liked the show so much they stayed for another show, missed the train back to their military post, and had to sleep that night on a marble floor in the train station. But after that interlude to work off some of the sweat and tears of months of training, Charlie and those on board with him were headed to France and war.

Following his first night's sleep aboard the now less-than-luxury liner, Charlie had made his way topside after breakfast to see the other ships in the convoy headed to England. Soldiers had seen training movies of the ships in convoy and the explosions that had occurred when German U-boats hit a cargo or troop ship with torpedoes. The threat from German U-boats was constant. To Charlie's surprise, he saw no other ships . . . the USS Wakefield was alone on the bounding sea, a rather unsettling feeling. As he began questioning a Navy crewman, the seaman said, "See that wake?" Charlie screwed up his face in a puzzled look. At that point in his life, the only wake Charlie could picture was the ritual surrounding the death of someone in his small rural community. The crewman went on to point out the rather unusual water trail (wake) created by the ship and explained how and why the ship altered its course precisely every eight and one-half minutes in a zigzag fashion to prevent U-boats from taking dead aim with torpedoes. Somehow the new knowledge didn't help Charlie rest any easier for the remainder of the sea-borne journey to the big port in England.

Two things did happen aboard ship that helped break the monotony of the journey and ease tensions just a bit. First, while wandering around amid the 9,000 troops, Charlie discovered to his surprise that his buddy, Ed Boling and his Army unit were also aboard. Second, the former heavyweight boxing champion, Jack Dempsey (now Lt. Commander, U.S. Coast Guard) was also on board and headed to England in connection with the Coast Guard's physical fitness program. Dempsey served as a referee in several "boxing matches" among the various soldiers. The fights were entertaining and helped relieve the tensions that were inevitable among 9,000 GIs headed into the unknown. One day, after having been taunted by a large, well-built soldier who wanted to box Dempsey, the former heavyweight world champion accommodated the man. They put on the gloves, entered the ring, the bell sounded and the match began. Dempsey threw the first and only punch and knocked the soldier out cold.

Amid the crowded conditions on the ship and the less-than-restful periods of sleep, Charlie found periods of time topside to reflect on the events that had brought him to this place at this time in his life. He remembered that crisp, sunny Sunday, December 7, 1941, and the afternoon spent playing "cow pasture football" on the football field at Madisonville High School. The game had ended around 4 p.m. A short time later, he and others in the small town of Madisonville had learned of the Japanese attack on Pearl Harbor, announced on every radio in the community. The problem was that not many knew where Pearl Harbor was at that moment in time. (Charlie would reflect many years later that "we were first-class isolationists.") In the wake of the attack, "blackouts" had been ordered in American cities and even rural areas. The Brakebill family had no trouble complying. They had two kerosene lamps, no electricity, no running water, and no phone. Charlie recalled Ed Smith, a local citizen, addressing an assembly at Madisonville High School a few days after the Pearl Harbor attack. Charlie was a senior at the time. Ed Smith's son had been among those listed as missing in action at Pearl Harbor (the son was later found alive). Charlie had gone on to graduate from Madisonville High School in May, 1942, and enrolled at the University of Tennessee in Knoxville during the first week of June.

Charlie had been influenced by a wonderful teacher of agriculture, Professor R. W. "Prof" Howard at Madisonville High School, and his intent was to graduate from the University of Tennessee and then teach Vocational Agriculture. When Charlie entered UT, the draft age was 20, and with a college degree, you could get a commission as a 2nd lieutenant in the U.S. Army. The summer of 1942 had gone well for Charlie at UT, but by the time he turned 18 on October 7, the draft age had been lowered to 18. At that time in America, now on a huge war footing, everyone was being drafted to serve one year in the military. Charlie remembered humming a few bars of "I'll be back in a year little darlin'," a popular song at the time. It did not take long for the United States to change the draft laws to include the phrase, "For the duration of the war plus six months." Charlie also remembered that "once your draft number came up, you went, period."

Charlie's roommate at UT was Phil Farris of Nashville. Phil's father had served as an officer in World War I and was still on active duty at the time. He advised his son and Charlie to enter the Enlisted Reserve Corps (ERC). On December 12, 1942, Charlie was sworn into the U.S. Army in the ROTC department located beneath the massive Neyland Stadium on the UT campus. He had remained a student at UT until mid-March, 1943. At that point, hundreds of UT students were being called to duty

"The burr haircut," Pvt. Charles Brakebill at age eighteen, Fort McClellan, Alabama, May, 1943

and Charlie had been ordered to report to Ft. Oglethorpe, Georgia on April 6, 1943, some sixteen months after the cow pasture football game.

He traveled to Chattanooga on April 5 and prepared for the short trip to Fort Oglethorpe, the next day. During the afternoon, Charlie and a small group of soon-to-be inductees had ventured out to ride the Incline Railway to the top of Lookout Mountain. At the top of the Incline, Charlie had met Ed Boling for the first time. It turned out Ed was a fellow UT student majoring in business. Also he met Paul McCammon, another UT student, and others. The following three weeks at Fort Oglethorpe had consisted of physical training exercise, the Army's famous kitchen police (K.P.) duty and picking up trash and debris around the base and barracks—just an introduction to the Army—not much in the way of preparing for war. Then it was on to Fort McClellan, a base near Anniston, Alabama. There, he and this new-found friend, Ed Boling, had pulled K.P. and guard duty together on several occasions. They were at an Infantry Replacement Training Center (IRTC). Here, new troops spent twelve-to-sixteen weeks in basic training followed by a ten-day delay in route to Fort Meade, Maryland, before being shipped to fight in North Africa. Charlie saw his first Germans at Fort McClellan—they were German POWs captured from among Rommel's Africa Corps in the fighting in North Africa. These were among Germany's elite troops and were impressive physical specimens.

Charlie thought about the "leave" he had gotten in August 1943 and the great visit he had back home with family and friends. (He learned later that when his parents saw him board the train in his hometown, his mother had fainted as the train left, and the fall had left her with a permanent scar on her face. Charlie often said he sometimes felt the families on the home front suffered more than sons in the military).

Upon his return to the base, he had received a message to go to the Orderly Room where the 1st Sergeant asked "do you want to go to ASTP?" Charlie remembered his first response was "I'll go anywhere but North Africa." Charlie entered ASTP (Army Specialized Training Program) and was bussed from Anniston to Tuscaloosa, Alabama, in early September 1943. He had taken a battery of tests at Tuscaloosa and was enrolled in some engineering courses. He had completed about two-and-a-half quarters at the University of Alabama by March 1944. It had been an interesting time at Tuscaloosa. Two of Charlie's closest friends, Ben Testerman, Jr. and Jack Banner had trained there as well, and had subsequently been shipped with others to the European Theatre as part of replacement units. Both were killed in action before Christmas 1943.

The majority of the group in Tuscaloosa had been shipped to the 106th Infantry in Camp Atterbury, Indiana, and then shipped overseas to Europe. While on the ship headed for Liverpool, Charlie had no idea what lay in store for that group of replacements for the 106th Infantry. Later, he found out that more than half of them were killed or captured in the Battle of the Bulge. Charlie had been assigned to the 1675th Engineering Utilities Detachment at Camp Claiborne, Louisiana, in April 1944. Again, fate stepped in and his now close buddy, Ed Boling, had been shipped to the same base with a Parts Supply Unit. Charlie and a team of men were building Bailey Bridges in Louisiana on D-Day, June 6, 1944.

Charlie had remained in Louisiana through mid-August, was granted a short leave home and then had taken a troop train to Boston. Ed Boling had been sent to Columbus, Ohio, but had shown up in Boston for assignment to Northern England as part of a Parts Supply Unit. They had once again said their goodbyes at the end of their Boston adventures only to "run into each other once again" aboard the ship as the USS Wakefield plowed on through the Atlantic Ocean toward Liverpool.

On September 21, two British destroyers came out to sea to escort the Wakefield into Liverpool. Escort destroyers were utilized to protect ships as they slowed while approaching the coastline, a necessary maneuver that left ships even more vulnerable to direct attacks by the Germans. There was a total blackout in Liverpool when the Wakefield docked at 1 a.m. on September 22, 1944. The troops immediately boarded a train for the twelve-hour ride through the blacked-out countryside to South Hampton, arriving there at 2 p.m.

Charlie's engineering unit immediately began boarding a small British ship which would take them across the English Channel to Normandy. Charlie was surprised when he looked back and saw his friend Ed Boling coming up the gang plank of the same small British ship. Ed Boling and his company were supposed to be headed to a Parts Supply Depot north of London!

Without good communications systems, such mistakes were common during WWII. Here was a company of 180 men specially trained to operate a depot in Northern England and now headed (erroneously) for Omaha Beach. Ed Boling's "lost company" faced many trials for the remainder of the war and never functioned as a parts supply unit.

Everyone was expecting a short voyage from South Hampton to Omaha Beach. But to their surprise, as the small ship neared the beachhead, waves were so high (8 to 10 feet) that the landing craft could not take them "from ship to shore." They were "on board" for the next 48 hours, just holding on and bobbing and weaving, amid violent bouts of sea sickness. When the channel waters calmed, they finally climbed down the rope ladders into the landing craft which took them ashore at Omaha Beach. On this particular day they did not see a German plane.

Charlie and Ed Boling said their goodbyes one more time (but did get together again in February or March 1945). Charlie's first view of Normandy was one that would stay with him for a lifetime.

Some three months after the bloody D-Day landings

by Allied Forces, the country boy who had grown up on a farm near Madisonville, was introduced to the grim realities of combat—the thousands of graves resulting from the Normandy invasion. Upon landing at Omaha Beach he walked up a steep hill spliced by high sand dunes. There, he looked out over 15,000 white wooden crosses of American graves on a sea wind-swept hill above the crystalline sands of Omaha Beach. There was no grass, no trees, just thousands of wooden white crosses with names and serial numbers of the dead, boys mostly, who would never get a day older. Many of them met their end on those beautiful beaches, the landing zones of the Allied Invasions that entered the lexicon of U.S. American military history as Utah and Omaha. "Wow! What an introduction to France," Charlie thought.

For the next two or three weeks, Charlie's unit remained in the Hedge Row country of Normandy waiting for their equipment (bulldozers, graders, dump trucks, etc.) to arrive. This time was uneventful for the most part. Charlie recalls that he traded sugar and coffee for some cheese in the little town of Montebourge. And, one day while wandering around, he saw a lady milking her cow and he wanted some fresh milk. He quickly learned to trade. For several mornings thereafter, he traded the lady either sugar, coffee, or cigarettes for a canteen—about a pint—of milk. However, upon his arrival one morning he found the lady "furious." She "cursed me out in what must have been several languages" as best as he could tell, and there was no milk to trade. Apparently some American soldiers had sneaked in and milked her cow the previous night. That was the end of Charlie's supply of fresh milk.

On October 7, 1944, (Charlie's 20th birthday), his

commander, Captain Harry Bloomfield (a UT alumnus from Memphis) asked Charlie if he would like to go with him to Cherbourg to check on the arrival of their equipment. At the time, Cherbourg was the only French port open for traffic; the other main ports heavily damaged by the Germans were being repaired.

On the return trip from Cherbourg, Bloomfield said he knew where they could get a real bath. That sounded good to Charlie—"what a birthday present." It turned out to be a portable shower unit with a two-minute water supply. It was Charlie's first shower in almost two months, and he got clean underwear and a fresh uniform.

In late October, 1944, Charlie's eighty-man Engineer Utility Detachment was assigned to duty in Rennes, the capitol of Brittany. They were there to support the 94th Infantry Division. One of the first things Charlie's unit did was post a 24-hour guard on the water point—this was a great supply of fresh water, a scarce item in a bombed out city—which needed "protection."

Letters sent "back home" were censored and soldiers were not permitted to tell family or friends where they were located. Charlie solved this problem by sending a series of letters in late October to his mother, changing the middle initial of his father's middle name in each letter home. Charlie's father's name was Alvin B. Brakebill, and most folks knew him as "A.B." (The first letter was to Mrs. Alvin R. Brakebill, the second to Mrs. Alvin E. Brakebill, the third to Mrs. Alvin N. Brakebill, etc.). His mother figured out this small code after the sixth letter in late October and knew Charlie was in Rennes. She contacted Ed Boling's parents who later informed Ed where Charlie was. That resulted in Ed Boling coming to Rennes in March or April 1945 for a visit.

Prisoners of War are a big problem when fighting a war. The Military Police were responsible for guarding German POws, and Charlie's unit and many other detachments worked and supervised hundreds of German POWs each day. A major task was building additional stockades for even more prisoners of war. Charlie was in charge of working a German POW crew one day when he learned his roommate Phil Farris was "missing in action." That day, the Germans didn't get a lunch break and Charlie momentarily hoped that at least one of the Germans might try to escape—he and his rifle were ready. (News arrived later that Phil Farris had been taken prisoner by the Germans December 1944, but was liberated on May 8, 1945).

Charlie's engineering detachment was also in Rennes to help get the city's infrastructure "back to normal." Their first assignment was to rehabilitate the hospital in Rennes. Members of Charlie's engineering detachment were sometimes separated, i.e., those operating road-graders or bulldozers might be in an area working on roads or airfields while the remainder of the group would be supervising German POW work units. The engineering detachment also worked in day and night shifts, seven days a week. Since supervising the German POWs was a somewhat regular occurrence, over time Charlie and the other GIs became a bit more familiar with some of the prisoners. Charlie recalled that some of the German soldiers had attended schools in the United States before the war and that some of them spoke English as

[14]

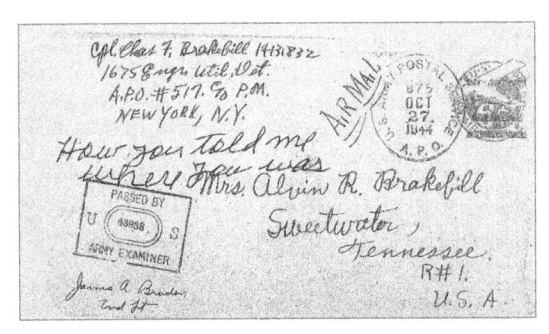

GIs were not permitted in their correspondence to tell family and friends where they were. Charlie solved this through a series of letters to his mother in late October, 1944. Charlie's father's name was Alvin B. Brakebill and most folks knew him as A.B. Charlie changed the middle initial of his father's name in each letter home, thus the first letter was to Mrs. Alvin R. Brakebill, the second to Mrs. Alvin E. Brakebill, and so on. After the sixth letter, his mother knew her son was in Rennes.

well as, or better than (at least grammatically) many of the GIs, and that among all the German POWs who were hoping to be liberated by the breakthrough at the Battle of the Bulge, there were many who were "just ready to go home." Some POWs would occasionally share a family photo with Charlie and the others.

In mid-November, Charlie's unit was assigned the task of replacing a roof on a large bombed-out building near the Rennes Railway Station. Once the roof was replaced, the building would be used by the military police. While working on this building, Charlie and other members of his unit saw a small group of people struggling to get a piano through French Doors in a second floor apartment, and they stopped work to assist. With the help of eight strong American soldiers the piano was hoisted up into the apartment with little difficulty. On this cold and blustery winter day was birthed "the Unfinished Romance of WWII" or as some of Charlie's buddies called it, "the piano love affair."

While getting the piano up to the second floor, Charlie met the Guillard family including the daughter, a beautiful girl with the equally lovely name of Anthelmette. Charlie also met her mother, father, and grandmother. Over the next few weeks, as the unit continued working on the bombed-shredded roof, Charlie got to know the Guillard family, and Anthelmette, gradually.

Anthelmette was a second-year pharmacy student at the Université de Rennes. Her family had left their home in the French port city of Lorient sometime during the early stages of WWII so that she might continue her education. Work on the roof continued and so did Sgt.

Charlie Brakebill (upper left) and part of the engineering unit at work repairing the roof of the bombed out building in Rennes, late October, 1944. It was from here that they saw a family struggling to hoist a piano up to the second floor of a small apartment building.

Brakebill's relationship with the Guillard family. Charlie admitted, "I didn't want the 'roof job' to be completed, so I slowed it down as much as possible."

Before the roof was completed, Charlie had developed a good relationship with the Guillard family. In addition to the father, mother, grandmother, and Anthelmette, another pharmacy student, Marguerite Josso, also rented space from the family in the small apartment.

Charlie's base was about two miles from the Guillard's home, so he tried to visit once a week. Charlie always made the trip on foot, both ways, sometimes in the rain and fog. Anthelmette spoke English, but her parents and grandmother did not. Charlie did not know what

The piano which Charlie and a crew of eight lifted to the second floor of the Guillard's apartment

her father did, or had done, as a career. He assumed they must have been reasonably well-off at one time and had sacrificed a great deal in moving from Lorient to Rennes so Anthelmette could continue her studies in pharmacy. Charlie and Anthelmette would often take a Sunday afternoon walk in a beautiful park in Rennes. The weekly visits were sometimes cancelled because Anthelmette took her studies seriously and needed the time to study. She would manage to get a note to Charlie whenever it was necessary to cancel a visit. There were never any picnics, and Charlie rarely ate a meal with the Guillards because food was scarce.

Christmas of 1944 was celebrated without much fanfare. All of the military units worked seven days a week in

January, 1945; Charlie and Anthelmette in Rennes. The snow covered roof in the background is the one Charlie's engineering unit replaced (Charlie is in work clothes).

Marguerite Josso (left), a friend and also a second year pharmacy student, and Anthelmette standing by the repaired roof. Marguerite rented a space in the Guillard home.

Anthelmette Guillard and Sgt. Charlie Brakebill in the Thabor Gardens in Rennes, May 1, 1945, seven days before WWII ended in Europe. This was the last photo taken of them together and was snapped by a passerby.

Anthelmette GUILLARD

says you "good night"
Her exam will not take place
the next saturday but
only the first March
or the five –

She hopes to see you
the next sunday night
and Bob also perhaps!
She is very sorry not to
ask you to come thurs-
day but I must study –
Good-night!

Anthelmette often sent messages to Charlie on the front and back of her personal card.

*Anthelmette on the way to pharmacy school,
January, 1945*

Photo at left is the Guillard's hotel in Lorient before WWII. Photo at right is the same building after Allied bombing in January 1943 (photo taken by a GI friend of Charlie).

twelve-hour shifts. Charlie remembered leaving the dining hall after the Christmas Day noon meal and looking up in the sky when he "saw something no one will ever see again." A massive formation of B-17 and B-24 bombers (a swarm better describes it) were flying directly overhead on their way to a bombing mission at the Battle of the Bulge.

Charlie had sent his parents photos of Anthelmette and told them of their relationship. Anthelmette wrote to Charlie's mother (at his encouragement) in Madisonville, and as familiarity bloomed, Charlie's mother sometimes sent the Guillards packages containing sugar, coffee, and chocolates, items very hard to find in war-torn Normandy.

Charlie's relationship with Anthelmette lasted from late November 1944 until Charlie sailed back to the United States in the summer of 1945. It was a deep friendship bordering on a romantic relationship. Anthelmette was a very nice young lady, a devout Catholic, and a very serious student. Charlie always assumed she was probably a year or two older than he, based upon her rank in pharmacy school. While many of the young French women were eager to attend a dance or social event sometimes held on the Army bases, Anthelmette always stayed away from such gatherings.

With the end of the war approaching, Charlie left Rennes in mid-April for a five day visit in Paris. He went alone, with just a few dollars in his pocket and a carton of cigarettes to barter. Parisians were ecstatic that the war might soon be over and were most gracious to Americans in uniform. GIs were required to wear their uniforms when traveling. Rooms and transportation were free to GIs in Paris. During his visit, Charlie saw most of the city's landmarks and a show at the Follies. He also saw the Glen Miller Orchestra (just a month or so after the death of Glen Miller). He sold the cigarettes (which cost GIs a nickel a pack) for a dollar a pack and made $18 in extra spending money. Aside from food, Charlie's only expense was the ticket to the Follies. (Anthelmette mentioned Charlie's trip to Paris in her letter to Charlie's mother dated April 26, 1945).

Rennes 26/4/45

Dear Mrs Brakebill,

I am very sorry you are not still received my first letter but the censor has perhaps stop it, or the ship, which transported it has not arrived in America.
It is a great pleasure for to write you again, though I don't speak and write well English. At first, I must thank you very much for the big packet that you sent to us by Charls. Please, you will write the price of it to Charlis to which we will pay. I should desire very much to thank you, by word of mouth, for your kindness, but, unhappily, the U-S is too far from France. My mother request to me to give hearty thanks to you for these good things which are very rare in France since this terrible occupation.
I have been very happy to know Charls. Every one here: my mother, my father, my good'mother my friends who are known him, and I will keep a good remembrance of him. If I did'nt know your most fervent wish was to see very soon him I should desire Charles to stay

[26]

here for a long time. My mother would desire to do more for him when he comes to my home but in spite of the liberation, the life in France is not as easy as before the war very many foods are still deficient.

Soon, I think, the peace will be... perhaps before you receive my letter!

The last week Charly had a fine stay in Paris but too short for visiting a so beautiful city. I should like for him to return for the parade of the 14th of July, the day of the French national feast which will be perhaps also, this year, the day of the parade of the victory!

I end here for beginning again to study my pharmacy which leaves me only a very few leisure hours.

I shall be very glad to receive a letter from you and have news of your home and family.

    Most sincerely
    Anthelmette

Here is my address:
  Mademoiselle A. GUILLARD
  8 bis Boulevard Beaumont
    Rennes (I et V)
   France

Anthelmette's letter to Charlie's mother, April 25, 1945

The war in Europe ended with the German surrender on May 8, 1945, better known as Victory in Europe Day, or "VE Day." Charlie knew that he would be going home, but didn't know when. He also knew the invasion of Japan was being planned, and that following a brief visit home, he and thousands of other soldiers returning from Europe would resume training and be part of the invasion of the Japan mainland. And, he knew if things somehow worked out for him, and he survived, he would be returning to UT to complete his education. Charlie had always leveled with Anthelmette about the future so the two never made any plans beyond the next visit or the next walk in the park. Charlie had hoped to stay in the "Army of Occupation" in Europe for obvious reasons, one being Anthelmette. He asked his commanding officer if he could remain in the Army of Occupation, but to Charlie's dismay, the request was denied.

Under different circumstances, Charlie could visualize that he and Anthelmette could be married, but he couldn't let himself get too serious about her. During the last few weeks in France, Charlie could tell Anthelmette was becoming more anxious about the relationship and this bothered him a great deal. A few days after May 8, Charlie learned his unit was scheduled to return to the United States. At this point, the young soldier far away from home made a mistake he was to regret every day for the rest of his life. In an effort to hurt Anthelmette as little as possible, Charlie thought the best thing for him to do was to make the break complete. He did just that.

During their last visit together on June 11, 1945, Charlie did not tell Anthelmette that he would be shipping out.

There was no final goodbye. For Charlie Brakebill, the

boy from Madisonville, he was leaving Rennes forever, and going home.

Charlie's unit left Rennes June 14 and sailed from the port of LeHarve June 21, 1945. The voyage home was uneventful, no zigzagging to avoid German U-boats, just a ship loaded with a few thousand GIs, many of them still recovering from wounds suffered in battle (but able to travel) and many liberated prisoners of war. Many of those on board had shaved heads and skin diseases, the results of lice infestations in the POW camps. All were grateful to have survived the war in Europe, and many were fearful of the invasion of Japan that lay ahead. Charlie's ship sailed past the Statue of Liberty at 7 a.m. the morning of July 4. Home at last!

Charlie had a couple of "real meals" and saw a new technological advance called television for the first time in the lobby of the Empire State Building during a two-day stay in New York. He then took a train to Camp Atterbury where he received a thirty-day leave and traveled back home to Madisonville for a celebratory reunion with family and friends.

Charlie learned of the Atomic Bomb dropped on Hiroshima, Japan, on August 6, 1945, while at home in Madisonville. In fact, he remembered that the main headline in the Knoxville newspaper had stressed the role Oak Ridge had played in developing the bomb. A secondary headline on page one identified "where" the bomb had been dropped. A second Atomic Bomb was dropped on Nagasaki August 9. The war was still on as he prepared to return to duty.

It was back to Camp Atterbury (briefly) and then a

*Sgt. Charles Brakebill, a photo taken
in Paris, late April. 1945*

train ride and transfer to Fort Belvoir, in Alexandria, Virginia, arriving August 12, 1945. The troops were there to begin intense training for the invasion of Japan. They even knew the date of the planned invasion: November 1945.

On the afternoon of August 14, Charlie and others hitchhiked their way to nearby Washington, D.C., and were having dinner at the Willard Hotel when a waitress

> RENNES
> JUNE 9, 1945.
>
> The pen is often said to be more powerful than the sword, but even with this great power it cannot sometimes express the things that are really in our hearts.
>
> Many miles of land and water can seperate us from the ones that we desire to be with, but we must always remember that we can never be seperated in our thoughts and prayers.
>
> —Charlie

A final note sent from Charlie to Anthelmette

shouted, (President) "Truman has announced that Japan has surrendered." Charlie and the others around the table jumped up from dinner and ran outside. "It was total bedlam" Charlie remembers.

The group worked its way (through a massive crowd of thousands) to Lafayette Park across from the White House. By this time, the buses and trolleys were stopped and completely blocked by human traffic. Charlie and

Anthelmette's last note to Charlie in France, June 10, 1945 reads "The remembrance is the presence in the absence, the voice in the silence, the endless return of a past happiness to which the heart gives the immortality." Her quote is attributed to French ecclesiastic, clergyman, journalist, and political activist, Jean-Baptiste Henri Lacordaire (1802–1861).

about forty other men and women in uniform climbed atop one of the buses near the White House fence and joined with the thousands shouting loudly, "Speak to us, Harry."

It was nearly dark when President Truman, joined by his wife, Bess and daughter, Margaret. They all left the White House and came outside to approach the gathering crowd. Truman thrust his arms upward and flashed "V for victory" signals to the crowd. About fifteen minutes later, most of the members of the president's cabinet came out to join the president. Other staff set up two ten-foot high speakers, with cables and a microphone so the president could speak to the crowd.

Charlie said it was one of the miracles of WWII that no one was killed or seriously injured during the celebration that night in D.C. The celebration continued all night. Charlie fell asleep in Lafayette Park, awoke at the "crack of dawn," and made his way back to Fort Belvoir at 6 a.m. He had been asleep in his uniform when Lt. Braden entered the barracks around 7 a.m. shouting "Let's go! Let's go!" The soldiers were assembled and ordered to go on a four-mile training march! When they reached their destination, they were shortly dismissed without explanation and marched back to the base.

Having witnessed the announcement of the end of WWII, and relieved that the planned invasion of Japan was no longer necessary, the GIs at Fort Belvoir nevertheless continued their intense training for the next several weeks. Much of the stress of the training was offset somewhat by the continued visits to D.C. in the afternoons and evenings. The many kiosks around the city continued to offer GIs free tickets to the latest movies on a "first-come" basis. And, the Stage Door Canteen was always open where good food was available.

Over time, Charlie's Engineering Detachment broke into smaller crews or units performing rather routine tasks on or near the base. The largest project undertaken by Charlie's small crew was the installation of a new air conditioning system in a base theatre.

On February 14, 1946, Charlie traveled by train from Fort Belvoir to Fort McPherson, Georgia, (near Atlanta), where he was discharged from the Army on Sunday, February 17. He rode a Greyhound bus from Atlanta to Madisonville. When the bus stopped at Stickley's Drug Store in downtown Madisonville (the town's designated bus stop), Charlie was still more than two miles away from his parent's farm with no prospects for a way to get there. He walked inside with his duffle bag and the first person he saw was "Prof. Howard," his favorite high school teacher. Prof. Howard said, "Let me give you a ride home."

The Rest of the Story

In all of the years I have known Charlie Brakebill (since 1970 when I began working for him at UT), I had never heard this story. In late fall, 2012, while visiting in Charlie's home, he was showing me some old family and WWII photos. And he told me about Anthelmette Guillard, a young second year pharmacy student in Rennes whom he began "courting" during 1944. His GI buddies had termed it "the piano love affair." Then he told me about (what he thought was) his failure to say a proper goodbye to Anthelmette when he left France in June 1945. This failure to say goodbye, and simply wondering what had happened to Anthelmette had bothered Charlie periodically for the almost seven decades since he had left France. In fact, Charlie had twice tried to learn what had happened to Anthelmette.

Charlie served in Germany with the Tennessee Air National Guard during the Berlin Crisis in 1961-62. At the end of the crises, he went to revisit Omaha Beach and the American Cemetery in Normandy. While there, he drove to Rennes to check with the college of pharmacy to see if there were any records concerning Anthelmette (no luck). Then again, in 1997, during a visit to Normandy, Charlie and his wife, Joyce (who knew the story) visited Rennes and the college of pharmacy in the hope of learning what might have happened to Anthelmette . . . again to no avail.

Charlie was hoping to bring some closure by having

me write a small book about this episode in his life. The book would include some letters, notes, and a few photographs of this very innocent love affair. The small book, to be self-published in some format, would be primarily for family members and perhaps a few close friends. Charlie's wife, Joyce had passed away in 2009.

Naturally, as I shared a draft of the story with Charlie, and as we did small edits here and there, we wondered if we could find out what might have happened to Anthelmette. There were many questions: did she graduate from pharmacy school?; did she marry and have children?; did she leave Rennes?; and, might she still be alive? In February 2013, I sent a detailed two-page letter to the college of pharmacy in Rennes briefly sharing this story and requesting any information they might share about Anthelmette, her graduation, or her family. I never received a written response, e-mail, or phone call from the university.

At the same time, and with some advice from others, I began trying to use the Internet to uncover French obituary notices or other pieces of information about Anthelmette. Again, to no avail. Then I spoke with a nice young man at Ancestry.com about our search. Helpful, "it might be possible," he said, but they primarily search genealogical records. And, it might be very expensive. I had all but given up hope of being able to find out what might have happened to Anthelmette Guillard.

One day in March 2013, I noticed an article and photo in the Knoxville News-Sentinel about the "Alliance Francaise de Knoxville." Paul Barrette, a member of the alliance, and a retired professor of French at the University of Tennessee, was in the photo. I called Paul, and explained the story and our attempts to learn what might have happened to Anthelmette. Paul was kind enough to invite Charlie and me to attend an upcoming luncheon in May at the French-inspired restaurant, Brasserie, and share the story with some attendees. Since the purpose of the meetings is to help people improve their French language skills and knowledge about the country, Charlie and I were at least a small distraction at the luncheon. But, all were gracious, and a few people were genuinely interested.

Valerie Read, one of the alliance members, told us her aunt, Marianne Depierre, was a retired journalist who lived outside Paris and might be able to help us. Valerie gave me Marianne's e-mail address, and I wrote a rather long e-mail to Marianne explaining the story more fully. She wrote back saying she would try to assist. A series of e-mail messages followed as I tried to provide the tidbits of information that might be useful. As it turned out, Marianne mentioned she knew a journalist and former colleague who was more familiar with records, obituaries, and government inquiries. "Give me three weeks to get back with you," she said.

In an e-mail about one week later, she provided the following information which a former colleague had found in a small obituary:

> *Anthelmette Guillard Letourneux was born on January 2, 1923, in Lorient and passed away March 1, 2007, in Vannes, France, a small coastal town near Lorient. She was 84. She was married in 1948 and had a son, Bernard Letourneux (wife, Maryse) and a daughter, Soazig (a lawyer married to Gilles Padovani, a film producer). There are six grandchildren.*

Learning that Anthelmette had apparently led a long and fruitful life brought a degree of closure for Charlie Brakebill. Thinking of life's odd coincidences, Charlie said, "My wife Joyce and I were married in 1948, had a daughter and son, and seven grandchildren ... Anthelmette was married in 1948, had a son and daughter, and six grandchildren. I'm pleased to have learned this much and am content to believe Anthelmette had a long and wonderful life." (At this time there was no thought of going to France for a visit).

> *As I write this on June 30, 2013, I'm hopeful that we may receive some additional information about Anthelmette. Marianne Depierre is attempting to write a letter, send an e-mail or contact the daughter, Soazig Padovani to explain this story and discover whether she or other family members might welcome a visit. Or, if Soazig would perhaps write a note about Anthelmette and answer a few questions that might help "fill in the gaps." If Marianne and her colleague are able to reach Soazig or another family member and we learn more, then perhaps the "rest of the story" can be more fully explained.*

Wonder of wonders! The next morning, Monday July 1, 2013, I opened my e-mail to discover a note from Marianne entitled "Good news for Charlie Brakebill." She wrote:

> *Dear Mr. Williams, dear Mr. Brakebill*
> *Full success! The bottle thrown into the Atlantic Ocean has arrived in the harbor! I found a contact address for Soazig,*

> *related the whole story and got the answer that she was very happy and touched.*
>
> *Charlie was very present in her family and they regretted to have lost contact. She has photographs, letters ... etc. Even Anthelmette's husband had told his wife to start research.*
>
> *They were married in 1948, were pharmacists in Sarzeau and then in Vannes for 40 years. The husband died in 1991.*
>
> *What a pity for all these lost years and occasions ... I suppose Valerie will also be delighted to learn that your encounter ended in a result.*
>
> *This was just a resume, Soazig will tell you more. (Here Marianne includes Soazig's address and e-mail address)*
>
> *I was happy to be able to push the bottle in the right direction. My "mission" ends here, but if you need me for further information, do not hesitate.*
> *Sincerely yours, Marianne Depierre*

I replied, "Charlie and I sincerely hope there may be more to the rest of this story."

In early July, I sent an e-mail to Soazig, Anthelmette's daughter, explaining my relationship with Charlie and the story I had written. A series of e-mails followed. Along the way, I kept Marianne Depierre informed of my contacts with Soazig. In addition, Charlie sent a handwritten letter to Soazig along with copies of some photos he had from WWII, and copies of notes Anthelmette had sent him and the letter Anthelmette had sent Charlie's mother. In late July, Charlie received a packet of photographs from Soazig. It contained some family photographs show-

One of Charlie's favorite photos of Anthelmette, taken on a beach circa 1951. Charlie had never seen this until Soazig, Anthelmette's daughter, sent him a copy during a period of correspondence before our trip.

ing Anthelmette and her husband, Bernard Letourneaux, Anthelmette's mother, and Soazig and Bernard, Jr. on vacation in other parts of Europe, and there were photos of Anthelmette in the late 1990s and early 2000s with some of her grandchildren.

One of the e-mails Soazig sent contained an old photograph of the piano. It seems the piano had been unused for a number of years and was in some disrepair. Soazig had sold it a few years earlier to someone for the parts. As our e-mail correspondence continued, I suggested that Charlie would consider visiting Rennes if such a visit was agreeable and could be scheduled. Soazig is an attorney working primarily out of her home. Her husband, Gilles, produces documentary films and his work requires him to make frequent trips to Paris and other parts of Europe.

Soazig seemed delighted by the possibility of a visit and we began to research possible dates. By now, we were in mid-August and Charlie and I knew that scheduled holidays are important to the French and other Europeans. We also knew that a visit would interrupt work schedules. And, Charlie and I wanted to be sure we could include a visit in Paris with Marianne Depierre and her husband during a trip to France.

Again through e-mail correspondence with Soazig and Marianne, we determined that a visit in late September and early October might be possible. I began working with my travel agent to arrange airline tickets to Paris, a car rental in Rennes, and a high speed TGV train from Paris to Rennes, our first major destination. Marianne pointed out that upon our arrival in Paris (early morning as it turned out), we should plan to check into a hotel and simply rest after the eight-hour flight . . . a great idea as it turned out.

Marianne reserved a room for one night for us at the Hotel Opera Marigny, a small hotel near the Church of la Madeleine and the Place of La Concorde. Soazig arranged accommodations for us in Rennes at the La Maison de Bertrand, a small apartment three blocks from her home. To accommodate our plans to visit Normandy and the various WWII sites during the latter part of our trip, Marianne made arrangements for us to stay at Les Chaufourniers, a bed and breakfast in Crouay, France, about six miles west of Bayeux.

Our travel schedule called for us to leave Knoxville for Paris on September 24, 2013 and return October 5.

Everything went as well as we might have hoped. We arrived in Paris at 7 a.m. on September 25. When Charlie stepped on French soil it was exactly sixty-nine years to the day that he had gone ashore at Omaha Beach as a nineteen-year-old soldier.

We made it to the hotel for a rest, and then in mid-afternoon, Marianne Depierre and her husband, Phillipe, met us at the hotel and took us for a walking tour of the Luxembourg Gardens and a driving tour of Paris. Charlie hosted them for dinner and we later watched the spectacular display of lights at the Eiffel Tower from the Alexander III Bridge over the River Seine. Our visit gave us the opportunity to thank Marianne for her efforts in locating Anthelmette's family and helping us with preparations for our trip. Marianne is the unsung hero in this story.

The next morning, we toured the area around the Place of La Concorde and visited the spectacular Church of la Madeleine. Charlie and I boarded the train in the afternoon for the trip to Rennes. The trip aboard the high speed TGV train was quiet and relaxing. We arrived in Rennes at 4:22 p.m. "right on time." We were met at the station by Soazig, her brother, Bernard, and his wife, Maryse. The next part of the adventure had begun!

We walked to Bernard and Maryse's apartment near the train station and enjoyed tea and treats before renting the car and following Soazig through the old section of Rennes to our hotel. Soazig had stocked the kitchen with juice, bread, jellies and jams, and coffee to see us through breakfast over our four-day stay.

Charlie and Marianne Depierre visit in the Luxembourg Gardens, Paris. Marianne and a former colleague had found Anthelmette's obituary for us. Marianne later contacted Soazig Padovani, Anthelmette's daughter, to tell her the story and of Charlie's search for information.

We were met at the train station in Rennes by Anthelmette's son and daughter. From left, Maryse and Bernard Letourneux, Charlie, and Soazig Padovani.

Soazig and Charlie visited as she led us to Thabor Gardens.

That evening, Charlie hosted a dinner for Soazig and her husband, Gilles, and Bernard and Maryse. During dinner Charlie presented Soazig and Bernard with gifts we had brought. These included books about Tennessee, the university, and other items which Elaine Meyer, president of the Museum of Appalachia in Norris, Tennessee, had given us for the trip. The conversation was lively and interesting as we exchanged stories and learned more about the Letourneux family and Anthelmette.

Charlie and I took a long walk through the older parts of Rennes on Friday morning, ending at the approximate location where Anthelmette's family's apartment building stood on the Avenue de Beaumont near the train station. A drive to St. Malo, and a walking tour of that ancient walled city completed a fascinating, and somewhat exhaustive day. Everywhere we walked that day, and particularly in Rennes, young people and old alike stopped to talk when they discovered Charlie was a WWII veteran. That proved to be the case for the remainder of our trip. To say that Charlie was overwhelmed by the warm reception he had received from all of Anthelmette's family would be an understatement.

Saturday and Sunday, September 28 and 29, were certainly highlights of our trip and indeed brought closure for Charlie. On Saturday, Soazig walked with us a few blocks to Thabor Park, the beautiful park where Charlie and Anthelmette often strolled during their Sunday afternoon visits in 1945.

The park is also the scene of the last photograph of the two of them together taken in May, 1945. Thabor Park is expansive and Soazig led Charlie to the wall where the original photograph of the wartime lovers was snapped.

Anthelmette's daughter, Soazig, with Charlie in Thabor Gardens in the approximate spot where Charlie and Anthelmette had been photographed in 1945. The benches are gone but the wall and the roses remain.

The park benches are gone but the wall and the roses remain, providing the backdrop for a photograph of Charlie and Soazig.

On Saturday evening, Soazig prepared a wonderful seafood feast in their home. In addition to Soazig and Gilles, Bernard and Maryse, four of Anthelmette's six grandchildren joined us for the evening. They included

Soazig and Gille's children, Elisa and Cesar Padovani, and Bernard and Maryse's children, Morgane and Guillaume Letourneux. Two of the grandchildren had traveled from Paris for the dinner. Charlie enjoyed the evening of stories and photographs, and learning more about Anthelmette's family. The warmth and hospitality made us feel like family.

On Sunday morning, Gilles and Soazig drove us to visit Vannes and Sarzeau. During the time in their car, we had an opportunity to learn more about Anthelmette' s life and career, and get answers to a few of the questions Charlie had always had. Charlie and I both had wondered why we couldn't get any information about Anthelmette through the University of Rennes where she had studied pharmacy. Soazig explained that during the time when Anthelmette was a student in Rennes, the final year of pharmacy had to be completed in either Paris or Marseilles. Anthelmette had transferred to the University of Marseilles in 1946 and completed her degree there. While studying in Marseilles, Anthelmette had met her future husband, Bernard Letourneux, who was two years younger and one year behind her in school. Bernard graduated in 1947 and they were married in 1948, coincidentally the same year Charlie had married Joyce Droke.

While Charlie had felt like part of Anthelmett's family during their courtship, and was on very good terms with her father, mother, and grandmother, he had never learned their names. Anthelmette spoke English, but her parents and grandmother did not, so the language barrier might have accounted for this. Soazig explained that

Soazig prepared a seafood feast and she and her husband, Gilles hosted a wonderful gathering in their home. Four of Anthelmette's six grandchildren were there (the other two are studying abroad). In a photo taken after dinner, from left: Cesar Padovani, Morganne Letourneux, Soazig and her brother, Bernard Letourneux, Charlie, Gilles Padovani, Elisa Padovani, Maryse Letourneux, and Guillaume Letourneux.

Anthelmette and her mother shared the same first names. In fact, both Soazig and her daughter, Elisa, share Anthelmette as part of their names.

During the afternoon Soazig also gave us more information about Anthelmette's parents and grandparents. Anthelmette's parents were Alfred Guillard and Anthelmette Brunier Guillard. Her paternal grandparents were Pierre Guillard, a baker, and Jeanne Allain, a cook. Anthelmette's maternal grandparents were Joseph Brunier, a stableman and later a jockey and trainer of horses, and Marie-Louise Auffret, a dressmaker. Soazig also told us Anthelmette's grandparents, the Guillards, had owned a hotel in Lorient which had been destroyed during Allied bombing attacks in WWII.

Following our visit to Vannes to see Anthelmette's home and the pharmacies she and Bernard had owned, we drove to Sarzeau to see their first pharmacy. We then visited the cemetery and Soazig led Charlie to Anthelmette's grave. Charlie placed a small container of roses on the grave and spent some time alone in reflection. While unspoken, I knew this small, but important journey had brought Charlie a moment of closure to this memorable chapter of his life.

*Charlie placing roses on Anthelmette's grave and pausing
for a few moments of reflection, September 29, 2013.*

Acknowledgments

When Charlie Brakebill asked me to write a small book about a very innocent love affair during WWII, it was to be a story just for his family. I made notes during a few visits, gathered his old black and white WWII photos and some letters, then turned the chronological facts into a story I hoped his children, grandchildren, and perhaps a few close friends would enjoy. It would be self-published and we might need 25 copies or so. No big deal, lots of folks do this regularly. Then, I started to try "just one more time" to find out what might have happened to Anthelmette Guillard. That led to the second part of the book, or " the rest of the story."

    I had exhausted all reasonable efforts in my search to determine what had happened to Anthelmette Guillard, when an article and photograph regarding the Alliance Francaise de Knoxville appeared in the Knoxville News-Sentinel in March, 2013. That caused me to contact Paul, Barrette, a retired UT French professor. He, in turn, invited Charlie and me to attend an upcoming meeting of the alliance where Valerie Reed suggested I contact her aunt, Marianne Depierre, a retired journalist living near Versailles. Marianne read the story and my e-mails and undertook the challenge to "find Anthelmette." Within a few weeks, one of Marianne's former colleagues had found Anthelmette's obituary from 2007. Marianne then contacted Anthelmette's daughter, Soazig Padovani, and told her the story. That led to our visit to France.

    To Paul, Valerie and particularly Marianne and her husband, Phillipe, we are most grateful.

In September, 2013 Charlie Brakebill and I traveled to France to meet Marianne in Paris and two days later, Anthelmette's family in Rennes. The warmth and gracious hospitality we experienced were beyond anything we could have imagined. Soazig and her brother, Bernard Letourneux, and his wife, Maryse, met us at the train station in Rennes. During the next three days, we also met Gilles, Soazig's husband, and four of Anthelmette's six grandchildren. We were treated more like family than new found friends, and we are grateful.

I have learned that publishing a book is far more involved than writing a book. Jim Johnston of Celtic Cat Publishing in Knoxville had too many projects on his plate to undertake the effort, but invited me to accompany him on a business trip to Nashville to meet his friend and publisher, Dariel Mayer of Periploi Press. Over lunch, she looked at the story and agreed to publish it. I am grateful to Jim for his willingness to help, and to Dariel for her extraordinary patience and skill in guiding me through the process.

I am also grateful to Fred Brown for his *Knoxville News Sentinel* story about "the piano love affair" in December of last year, and for reading a final draft of the book and writing its foreword; to Kristin Williams for designing the cover; and to Michael Stinnett and his colleagues at the Antique Piano Shop for providing a French piano very much like the one that started this story to be photographed for the cover.

Thanks to Thompson Photo of Knoxville for copying and digitizing the black and white photos, letters, and notes from Charlie's files, and to Elaine Meyer, president of the Museum of Appalachia for providing some gifts and books to share with our new-found friends in Rennes."

—Jack E. Williams
October 2014

Charlie Brakebill is Vice President for Development Emeritus at the University of Tennessee. Following service in WWII, he graduated from UT in 1948, taught Vocational Agriculture in high school, and was re-called to active duty during the Korean War. He then worked as Sales Mgr. for Bacon Ice Cream Co. He joined the Tennessee Air National Guard and was again called to active duty when the Guard was deployed to Ramstein Air Force Base in Germany during the Berlin Crisis. While in Germany he served as Executive Officer for the 450 Guardsman called to duty. In 1962, he was recruited by UT president Dr. Andy Holt to help build the newly formed fundraising program at the University of Tennessee. He worked for the UT System from 1962 until his retirement in 1996. Working with Dr. Ed Boling and Dr. Joe Johnson, he helped develop UT's fundraising programs state-wide and on each campus, built a successful deferred giving program, and helped guide a number of successful campaigns. Throughout his career, he emphasized, by example, the importance of building relationships in order to secure major gifts. He and his wife Joyce had been married 62 years when she passed away in 2009. They have two children, seven grandchildren, and four great grandchildren.

Jack Williams is Vice President for Development and Alumni Affairs Emeritus at the University of Tennessee. A native of Knoxville, he graduated from UT in 1964 with a B.S. degree in History. He worked with the federal government and in the business sector before joining the University of Tennessee as Director of Special Gifts in 1970. In 1977 he became Director of Development for UT, Knoxville, and was named Vice Chancellor for Development and Alumni Affairs in 1981. He served in that role until being named Vice President for the UT System in 1997. He retired in 2006 after 36 years with UT. He is an avid photographer and serves as an advisor or board member to a number of nonprofit organizations including Friends of the Smokies, the East Tennessee Historical Society (past president), and the Museum of Appalachia. He and his wife Carolyn have two children and five grandchildren.